ABANDONED SOUTHERN MINNESOTA

JULIE BRONSON

AMERICA THROUGH TIME®
ADDING COLOR TO AMERICAN HISTORY

America Through Time is an imprint of Fonthill Media LLC
www.through-time.com
office@through-time.com

Published by Arcadia Publishing by arrangement with Fonthill Media LLC
For all general information, please contact Arcadia Publishing:
Telephone: 843-853-2070
Fax: 843-853-0044
E-mail: sales@arcadiapublishing.com
For customer service and orders:
Toll-Free 1-888-313-2665

www.arcadiapublishing.com

First published 2019

ISBN 978-1-63499-175-9

Typeset in Trade Gothic 10pt on 15pt
Printed and bound in England

CONTENTS

ACKNOWLEDGMENTS

I would like to begin by thanking the people who helped make this book possible. First, my husband, Doug, for putting up with my endless hours staring at the computer screen and pecking away at the keyboard. Second, my friend, LeAnn Trolen, for always being ready to go on an adventure with me to find new abandoned treasures to photograph. Third, my friend, Susie Crane, who helps make sense of my ramblings by correcting and clarifying things I sometimes have a hard time putting into words. And finally, Tess Kauffmann for helping find mistakes I overlook even after rereading things a hundred times. Thank you all for being there for me.

INTRODUCTION

If you picked up this book or bought it online, it means you must have an interest in old abandoned dwellings. I will show a few of them in my neighborhood and within a few miles from my home. Along with the photos, I hope to give you an idea of the feelings these places bring out in me. I believe you will understand how it feels to be pulled in as they beckon to me as I drive by, begging for me to take a photo or two so they will never be forgotten.

The first abandoned photos I took were way back before digital. I don't even know where those photos are, but I do remember how expensive it was to have them developed. The wait was miserable. The house was a big two-story on the edge of town that you could obviously tell vagrants lived in from time to time. I wasn't scared at the time to go in by myself, but the way times are now, I don't think I would do it today. I knew the house was about to be torn down, so I wanted to get in and get shots of it first. I called the realtor on the "For Sale" sign to get permission to go in. I have been allowed to do this many times since then and will continue to ask when I know a place is about to disappear. I am not as interested in trying to get super creative shots, I just want to show how sad and beautiful the decay is. I also document the disrespect felt by vandals, their pathetic need to deface these places by spray painting nasty words on once-beautiful wallpapered walls and broken furnishings.

Sounds of silence from an old piano.

ABANDONED SOUTHERN MINNESOTA

To begin, our journey takes us to the farm, places where self-sustaining farmers and their entire family helped make a hard life a joy to live. They had huge gardens and cellars to store the fruits of their labor. Many of the houses are too rundown to set foot in. A fall through the floor would not be good. Lots of the photos I take are from the vantage point of a missing window or doorway. I always respect the dreaded "No Trespassing" sign, but will see if there might be a neighbor close by that knows the owner, to get permission to enter. The ones with those signs are obviously the most enticing! I have been asked a few times what I am doing, but having a copy of the books I've published seems to be all that is needed to get people to open up and tell me about the place and send me in the direction of more treasures to photograph. Even they have overlooked the beauty of the place they farmed around for many years. Perhaps this is why so many of the homes I find end up abandoned. A farmer will buy up the land around the acreage and rent the house for a while until the insulation has settled in the walls so badly it is too expensive to heat. It is hard to find a renter that wants to stay, so the house gets locked up instead of fixed up. Eventually the vandals make their way in and trash the place, leaving broken windows and doors open for critters big and small to come right on in. The rain, wind, and snow take this opportunity to enter too. That's when the process of rot begins. A tree will fall on the roof, leaving a hole, or the wicked wind will blow shingles off, exposing very old wood, and the decay starts there too. Wood begins to get wet and soak one board, then the next, then mold grows and turns black, eating away at the wood. Once weakened, the weight of the wet wood in the walls begins to bear down on itself. After many years, it finally folds under the pressure. Trees that love growing right up next to foundations push their way in from the outside, making it that much easier for the load bearing walls to fall further into the basement. Mother Nature is an expert at reclaiming what is hers, even though it is a mighty slow process.

In southern Minnesota, there are many of this type of home. I have revisited my favorites over time and am heartbroken to find a few have been torn down, or arsonists have taken them away from us. There are a couple I look for every day as I drive to work. If I don't see them right away, my heart falls into my stomach.

Trees grow too close to foundations and win the battle. This house is gone now.

I'm not sure what this little building was in Alma City, MN.

House in Alma City, MN.

What is left of a door on what appeared to be a general store-type building in Alma City, MN.

When I see a big digger sitting in front of a place, or the trees have all been taken down and shoved up around the house, I know yet another one is doomed. One such time I visited one of my favorite houses and found the trees were pushed up to the house on all sides. I had heard in the past that this particular house was haunted. I am not convinced as to whether this is possible or not so as I was walking around taking photos, I said out loud to the possible occupants that I was very sorry their home was being taken away, and there wasn't a thing I could do about it, but if they chose to ride along with me to another place to take up residence, they were more than welcome to do so. Of course, I don't really know if they did or not, but I felt I had done my part. A short time later, I took a drive out there again and there wasn't even a trace of the home that once was there. The barns and sheds were gone, along with the old truck that was an important part of the old farm. Where once stood a thriving farmstead covered with mighty trees, a huge old four-square house, and at least four other buildings, there was only bare land, cleared for just another few acres of corn or beans.

House near Buford, MN. It appears to be destined for fire or dozer in the near future.

Up in flames. Training for the fire department. This house was half of a house. The other half was across the road. It was a huge house to that was split in to two homes.

Above: I'm not sure why people keep houses instead of knocking them down. There was a new house just a few steps from this one. I like to think it is kept because of sentimental reasons.

Left: Colorful vines hug a house.

This is one of the first schoolhouses in Freeborn county. It was near Myrtle, MN. It is gone now.

This barn seems to be screaming "Whoa!"

The red vines caught my eye for a unique way to frame the barn. It, too, is gone now.

This is one of my first favorite finds. The story is that a man had this house built and furnished for his bride-to-be. She backed out of the wedding and no one moved in. There were a few renters over the years, but no one ever really called it home. It was burned by arsonists last winter.

I can see this house from the freeway every day on my way to and from work. It gets pretty swallowed up by vegetation in summer, but I can still see it. The foundation is giving way under it so I don't know how much longer it will last.

Fancy trim around the doors and windows found in many old houses.

Rusty roofs are much better than no roofs!

Gravity winning.

Silos used to guide a traveler home. Artistic marvels.

Rusty silo top with a sign to cover the hole that the sileage blower was poked in through. Much prettier from the inside than the outside.

Green seems to have been a popular color.

Porch trim on an old schoolhouse.

Wide open for all to enter.

Seeming to scream.

Peering in through the windows, I saw the floor was about 4 feet from the ceiling. They were collapsing together.

Sturdy barn with nothing to do.

Yes, there is a house in there. But it is long gone now.

Barn slowly giving up the fight.

This barn gave in and laid down. I wonder if it made any noise.

House by Wells, MN. Gone now.

Snowy granary.

At the west end of the road I live on, there was a farm on a hill. A house was there when I first moved here, but back then I didn't yet have a fascination for these old houses like I do now. I still regret not going up and taking photos of it while it stood there. On this same acreage there were beautiful giant oak trees and the tiniest new trees growing from acorns. They show us life is meant to go on. There was also a beautiful glazed salt-brick silo and a ratty old windmill. I stopped up there to take photos of them quite a few years ago and was very surprised and excited to see inside to the top of the silo, which was also brick. It was beautiful! I took a few pictures of it, and decided it looked like an eye. The sun was in just the right spot when I was taking photos of the windmill and I got the neatest sun star. I hurried home to see my pics on the computer and was giddy with the excitement of catching that sun star, but the photos of the silo top were even better. I printed it out on photo paper, and that looked good, but it looks amazing on canvas. The sad part is now the entire place on the hill is gone. It was always a landmark for coming home. Now I nearly drive right on by my turn on the way home. I almost can't bear to look in that direction. It is a terrible loss for me.

My first silo "eye." The silo is long gone now, but it opened my eyes to this hidden beauty.

On almost every country road, you will come upon at least one place human inhabitants have vacated. Usually, the land was sold to a farmer, or the people who lived there moved to town or a nursing home, or they may have even passed on. Whatever the case, the last one to leave and turn off the lights could not have known the sad state in which these once beautiful homes would fall into.

Torn curtains fly in and out of busted windows until only strings of thread remain. Curtains so proudly picked out and ordered or stitched together by hand wave to people that pass by as if trying to attract attention to the house. It is as if they are motioning for strangers and friends alike to come in and sit for a cup of coffee and to give them a break from the deafening silence.

Beauty in the details. The gingerbread and the torn curtains are such a contrast.

I call this one Grandmas Kitchen, because if you look close you can almost see her in the chimney.

Creamery in Alma City, MN.

Pretty window trim.

One can almost hear the laughter of the children who once swung on this small swing set.

Half a barn.

My friend's summer kitchen.

Can you imagine sitting out in the rain on that porch? I can.

Basement walls gone. House struggling to stay up but too weak to hang on.

I'm not sure, but this appears to have been a school. It has a newer foundation. It hasn't been abandoned too long.

This is the house my mother and aunt lived in when they were young in New Richland, MN. It is gone now.

I love this old house. From the upstairs window, you can see and hear the creaking of the windmill as the wind slowly turns it. How wonderful it would have been to fall asleep to that music every night.

This house was packed full of treasures we could see through the lost windows. It also had patches on it made of soup can bottoms. It was taken down a few years ago.

This house near Walters, MN, had old ceiling tin tacked up around the foundation. I imagine it was for rodent control.

Some of the old houses were once log cabins. The owners would add rooms and they would put siding over the logs to match the newer part of the house. You wouldn't even know the logs were there until the outer siding starts to slip away or the paneling on the interior walls begins to warp and fall away from the logs. There is a house west of me exactly like that. The logs are starting to show up very clearly now. It has been sitting empty for almost forty years. The windows have all been busted out by vandals. The floor is beginning to cave in. In a few years, it will be gone. I was told it was a post office at one time, but there is no trace of it.

Above: You can't tell from this shot, but the part with the green mossy roof is a log cabin—so much history left to rot.

Right: Logs in the walls of previous photo.

When my husband and I were about to be married, we were told we could stay in this house until we found a place of our own. We cleaned it up and began to move some of our things in. There was even a dishwasher in this house! I never used a dishwasher before so one of the first things I did was load it up with the dishes that were left in the cupboards. We didn't have any "real" dishwasher dish soap, but we did have liquid. I figured since it was the wrong stuff, I better use extra. I filled the little soap dispenser and shot a good stream of soap in on the dishes. Well, you can possibly imagine where this is going. We started it up and it wasn't long before we had suds seeping out. This quickly turned into a whole lot of suds! What a mess. The floor was entirely covered with bubbles. We were laughing, scooping and sweeping suds out the door.

We ended up not living there after all. The lady who owned it changed her mind when we were away on our honeymoon. I would have really appreciated that house and it would have been restored to a log cabin if we had been able to buy it. I tried to find a buyer for the logs in it, as with a couple of others in the area, but there is just not enough left of them to bother with, I guess. It does make one wonder how many of the homes we see are log cabins in disguise.

A few years ago, I thought I spotted an eagle headed that way, so I hopped in my car and made a mad dash for the place. I parked at the end of the long driveway and walked up with camera in hand. I figured if I sat quietly, I could get a good shot of the eagle when it came back. I sat waiting and heard some rustling. I looked up at the roof of the house where there were holes in the shingles. Before long, a mother raccoon came out and behind her were three babies following in a line. I could not believe it! I was thrilled to pieces. I got a few shots of them before they shuffled back down the hole in the roof. I worried about the babies being fair game for the eagle, but before I left, the bird I followed showed up. It ended up being a turkey vulture. I was relieved for the kits.

Houses once proudly kept painted with lawns neatly trimmed are totally cloaked in vegetation in the summer. The mosquitos and itch weed, as well as the raspberry thorns, make exploring them nearly impossible, which is why so many of my photos are taken in fall, winter, or early spring. Quite a few homesteads are nestled up at the end of a long driveway that is either grown over with brush or blocked by fallen trees—or possibly the farmer has gotten rid of the driveway completely to plant another acre of corn.

Framed in Phlox.

This house is a long distance from the road, but it appears to have someone that mows around it for us to get a good picture or two.

House turned chicken house.

Near the small town of Hope, MN.

Trees for company.

Here is a unique way to take down a house. Just use a saw and cut it in half!

Used for target practice.

Treasures left behind.

This appears to have been a school made into a home.

Silo top that looks to me like a star filled night.

Not too sure what this is, but love the textures.

Somehow the old car near this house made it look even lonelier.

Pink barn somewhere near Rochester, MN.

This beautiful barn appears to have had the ground beneath it sink so the back half of it also sunk. One would have thought it would break instead of bend.

Above: How much is that kitty in the window?

Left: When I first looked at this, I thought it was a driveway that led up to the side of the barn. But it is the rest of the barn that fell away from the standing section we see. Funny how the foundation on this side still looks perfect.

Above: Lovingly protected by windbreaks of trees.

Right: There were still sheep living in thc basement of this barn when I took this, but it was taken down by time a short time later. The sheep are okay!

During a photoshoot, my friend, LeAnn, and I headed up to Waseca, because she had spotted a house she wanted to investigate closer. When we get to a new place, she goes one way and I go the other and we meet up in the middle to tell each other about the things we've seen and to point out whatever needs to be photographed. A short time after we split, I heard her shriek. As she rounded the corner of the house, a turkey vulture that was sitting in the window had taken flight and scared the dickens out of her. I don't know if anyone reading this has ever been up close to one of those huge birds, but they are extremely intimidating and make a lot of wind noise when taking off. That got her heart pumping for sure!

Vulture house near Waseca, MN.

Roof gone. I love how you can see trees and sky through the upstairs window.

Beautiful green trim near Myrtle, MN.

Time worn paint on wainscoting.

This was falling backward into itself. You can tell by the roof boards moved forward. It was pretty much all that was left of this house.

New use for an old house: horse house.

Cleverly tagged with "Die" by vandals.

Left: Taken from a missing window. If you listen closely you can almost hear the footsteps.

Below: I wish I could have seen this when the little entry roof was still in place.

Built-in cupboards going down with the house.

Something was missing, but I couldn't tell what.

This house near Albert Lea, MN, belongs to a friend of mine. He let us go in a few years ago to take pictures. There was still electricity at that time. The huge attic had been home to bats for a long time, as there was an extreme amount of guano and the odor was nearly unbearable. He told us they used to roller skate in the long upstairs hallway.

Barn in the trees. One of the first I photographed when this journey began. Near Keister, MN.

Right: One of many fancy doors.

Below: We noticed the awesome details of this house as we were passing by and had to stop in. Luckily, the owner was on his way in with a tractor to cut the grass, so we got to visit and take as many photos we wanted.

Another apparent schoolhouse.

You could not tell from the front, but once around to the side you could see there had been a fire.

The colorful elevator in Walters, MN.

Crumbling elevator.

Lawnmower storage. It had many push-behind mowers inside.

Do these houses enjoy my visits? Can they sense my presence and wonderment with them as much as I can sense the flow of emotion radiating from them? I believe they do. I admire with as much time as I can give them. This is probably much more than they have received in the past twenty, thirty, forty, or more years. I take in all the details that were once things neighbors came over to see when the house was first built. I love to run my fingers over the trim and siding so carefully painted. I admire features that set it apart from the neighbor's house up the road—an extra carved piece of trim in a corner, oak baseboard patterned to match the ceiling trim, the newel post with an extra ball to top it off at each end of the stairs. There are houses with an extra half story and closets with secret doors to crawl spaces used to hide valuables such as a special music box with the ring that Grandma had, or the earrings that a favorite aunt left. Boxes full of Christmas decorations and the handmade wooden box that held Grandpa's service uniform and medals are stashed safely behind the secret doors. Hidden away in dusty attics are trunks full of old clothing smelling of ancient mustiness and photos with names and dates penciled on the backside of relatives no one would remember if not labeled. Imagine the looks on the faces of children snooping in an old trunk when they happen upon a photo of a person in a casket. Some families used to take pictures of deceased loved ones. The house I grew up in had hidden doors in the closets like that. Part of the floor had boards to walk on, but the other part was just the joists and insulation, so you had to be really careful when sneaking around in there.

Right: Cheerful and sunny on the inside!

Below: I don't often turn photos to black and white, but the lighting in this room begged me to do it.

These houses would pour out their stories if only a person could hear them speak. They wait in eager anticipation with all the love, hate, sadness and happiness held within their quiet walls for a visitor to come along who can feel their emanations. If a person could hear what they are trying to say, they each could write a book of their own. Stories of the baby just conceived, and the baby just miscarried, would be written on the same wall as the husband and wife who fought about not having enough money for another child but were still happy about the news that one was on the way. Stories of kids coming home with an award for winning the spelling bee and the boy whose pa grounded him because he forgot it was his turn to milk the cows. There would be news that big brother was sweet on the girl with long red braids and she was making eyes right back at him. I listen, and yes, I believe these houses like my company. I let them know they are not forgotten.

There are a few places that have two houses on one bit of land. Sometimes a new house gets built and the old house gets left standing because it is a good place for storage, but no one takes care of it any longer like they used to. Windows get broken and covered with plastic or a piece of plywood (if anything at all). Before long, the house no one loves anymore weakens. The floor starts to sag from the weight of storage and lack of care. The floor falls in and valuable items stored there slide into the basement.

I was born and raised just a few miles northwest of where I live now. When I was growing up, we had another house on the homestead. We always called it the "yellow house" because it was well ... yellow. My folks lived in it until they had the "red" house moved to the property from a few miles away. I remember storing stuff in the house and the renters who lived there. The most memorable one was a trapper that would occasionally show up. I only remember his fridges full of fur. That memory still haunts me even though I was very young at the time. This could be one of the reasons I am a vegetarian! I very often have dreams about the yellow house. I wish I had a picture of it. I also remember vaguely that my grandma lived there. She taught us the song, "Make the World Go Away." I remember seeing a photo of her on the front step watching for the school bus with us. I wish I could remember more. The yellow house is gone now. I don't even know when it disappeared.

Another common practice in this area is the use of old houses for fire department training. I am glad they get to train but am extremely sad to see them use my beloved old houses for the fires. I have many photos of them going up in flames. The heat is extreme and as the paint bubbles and melts off the trim, it is as if the house is crying. Memories both good and bad are left in a pile of smoking ash and embers.

Windmill trapped by trees.

Railroad car on my great grandparent's farm near New Richland, MN.

The house my great grandfather built at the turn of the century, around 1899 or so. Near New Richland, MN. It is gone now.

Yet another totally different style of house.

I like to be able to use a barn window as a frame for a shot.

Hen house?

The porch in this house had a beautiful lamp and sheer curtains. You could tell it was well loved.

The elements are taking her back to the earth.

Railroad car near Clarks Grove, MN, full of used lumber and building supplies. It is long gone now.

Patches made from soup cans.

Left: Weeds growing up between the glass.

Below: Reflection of the windmill makes it look like two windmills, but there is only one.

Above: Outside view of Grandmas Kitchen house.

Right: Standing inside the old hog house made for a great frame for this house shot. This place is now a field. Can't even tell there was a farm place.

The fanciest siding I have ever seen on an old shed. It was ceiling and wall tin that must have been salvaged from another old building.

This house is the one with the staircase also in this book. It was being used as storage. There is also another newer house on this acreage.

Above: Many houses have been added on to. Quite a few of the additions crumble first.

Right: A missing staircase in the house on the cover. The house is gone now.

Crumbling granary.

One of the houses they trained in was home for many bats. Now I don't know about you, but I love bats. They eat mosquitos. As the house filled with smoke, the bats began to emerge. Some waited until it was too late and ended up burned very badly. I didn't have the heart to do it myself, but had a big tough guy come step on one right there in front of me to put it out of its misery. I wonder how many others lost their home or their life that day. That is just another good reason to leave these grand old homes standing. The house was not in that bad of shape and it was huge. The people passed away and no one in the family wanted to take on the old house, but the boys wanted to keep the rest of the farmstead in use because one of them lived across the road. He grew up in that big house. I would not have been able to let it go if it were me. The entire family who grew up there was witness to the fire. There were lots of tears shed that day.

I have spoken enough about the homes that have been taken away. Let's focus now on the ones we still get to see. Not everyone sees abandoned places in the same way. These places have different meanings to different people. If a place was once a thriving business that closed and the building is only used for storage now, I consider that abandoned. There should be daily activity in a structure to keep it alive.

Multiple homes have renovations started that come to a halt for one reason or another. Perhaps there was an illness or an injury that stopped construction. Maybe the owner lost their job and ran out of funds. Whatever the case, the new sheetrock and two-by-fours on the walls or stacked as if ready to use have gone to waste, same as the rest of the house.

There are also houses that only appear to be abandoned. I can't tell you how embarrassing it is to drive up a long driveway because you've seen what looks like an old abandoned shack, only to have some old grisly looking guy come out to ask what the heck you are doing. It was hard to explain to him that I thought his house looked abandoned. I hightailed it right out of there with my tail between my legs.

There are also many barns in my area that are abandoned. At least some are still standing, so we can see a bit of construction from the past. A few are barely holding themselves up and some are in the beginning stages of final decay. The first noticeable thing is a patch of shingles missing. Then there is a slight hole that appears in the roof. Then the hole becomes larger and the area around it starts to sink in a bit. Once this happens in a big enough area, the weakness spreads and in a short while, an entire part of the roof caves in. In another case near me, the barn boards near the foundation began to collapse and the poor old barn fell to its knees before crumbling. It is interesting to watch the sad progression in both cases. There have been at least ten barns that I have been able to watch as they slowly dissolved in my short fifteen-mile trek to work every day for the past thirty-nine years. Each one is just a little bit different in the way it collapses, but just as sad. Mammoth-sized barns that once housed the livestock seem to wither away once the horses, cows, and pigs move out. It is as if the life inside the barn was breathing life into the barn itself. Once gone, the sounds and smells fade away. Hay in the loft becomes home for many scurrying creatures. Cats, raccoons, mice, rats, woodchucks, skunks, and birds move in in droves to take up housekeeping. Deer wander into the lower part for shelter in the summer from rains and in the winter from snow and biting winds. Occasionally people will decide to help themselves to the barn wood that has become so popular for many craft projects. I wonder how many basement bars have barnwood as decoration and I also wonder how many of them discovered that once in an enclosed area like that, the smells of the barn aren't really gone after all! Cupolas from the tops of the barns are a popular garden decoration, and luckily, many of them have been saved. Sometimes the bullet holes from target practice add to their charm.

Colors on the old barns fade over time. Once, a bright red barn painted over by white in later years had faded it becomes a delightful shade of pink. Mostly they turn gray, beautiful soft shades of gray. Wood grain, either smooth and mellow or grainy and harsh, shows up nicely in a good rain. The colorful lichen adds to the color pallet.

Along with the old houses and barns, I run across old swing sets tangled in the weeds while waiting for the next kid to come along and hop on to go for a ride. If not held down by weeds, the swing gently sways in the breeze, making a sad squeaking sound where the chain link rubs the bar.

There are also many windmills left standing in farmyards where the well used to be or sitting out in the middle of fields and along fence lines. With some, it's a wonder how they can even be standing because they are so ratty. Their bars jut out in every direction with blades missing or ripped in half and bullet holes, lots of bullet holes! Windmills are extremely popular targets. Some of them still work, singing a mournful song as the wind slowly turns their blades even though they aren't pumping water like they were intended to do so long ago. Some windmills are swallowed up by neighboring trees. The trees grow wherever they want, and the windmill, trying to turn, gets tangled in the branches. In some cases, vines grow all the way up to the top as well, choking out the turning mill. Headless windmills

Lichen covered siding bowing in the wind.

are also very common. The tops got taken down for some reason or possibly have fallen on their own. They make beautiful garden ornaments if saved and attach nicely to the side of a barn.

The only thing left standing in some farmyards is a silo. The roofs are mostly gone, having fallen in or blown away many years ago. Some turn themselves into big planters and from a distance you see a tree emerging. Most of the silos were made of salt-glazed bricks or cement. Like I mentioned before, if you look up inside the brick ones, you would swear an artist was at work when they made the very top. Some of the tops were made of wood or tin and, if intact, are fine works of art. Few complete silos are standing that were made of wood. No matter what they are constructed of, I don't think any of them are used to store silage anymore. Some are used as a burning pit or just a place to throw dead branches and grass clippings. Many have weeds growing in them. I have seen a few with skeletons of critters that got in and couldn't get out. That is very sad. One place I visited had more than one skeleton, so I looked around until I found a stick to put in there that would be strong enough for a small critter to climb back out if it wanted to.

The wind is winning against this windmill.

The windmill makes this house look so tiny near Clarks Grove, MN.

Right: The vines climb up to reach the sun.

Below: The view from the underside of a topless windmill.

Left: Tree in a silo. We could see this from the road, and it drew us in.

Below: Staples of the farm. Silo, windmill, and granary.

There are many corn cribs/granaries still standing as well as silos. They have slatted boards so the corn can breathe. The corn was stored on the cob or it would have run out the slats. These cribs aren't used as intended anymore either. Most of them are just storage. People have so much stuff! Many storm windows and screens seem to find their way to cribs, but they too don't stand a chance against the rain, snow, and wind Mother Nature sends in. Tractors, corn pickers, hay rakes, and wagons of all sorts get parked under the roofs of these sheds, but one wonders if it would have been safer to park them out in the middle of a field instead of in a place that had the very real potential of caving in on the implement. I also think the person that parked it there the last time really intended to use it again.

There were so many interesting textures on this old granary.

Wagon storage.

There wasn't even a thought of abandoning it forever. It somehow just ended up that way through no fault of their own.

On occasion I have run across an old house that has been turned into a barn. One such house actually started out life as a log cabin. It was used for many years, then moved out of the way to make room for a bigger, better house. Then additions were added to create a barn with cattle stanchions and all. Hay was stored in it until the upper floor caved in and the whole thing started to go wonky. The nails used in the construction were old square nails. I tried to get a good shot of them for you to see. I was lucky to get photos of the place before they pushed it down and buried it. There is another one just a few miles east of me that was turned into a horse barn. They cut a hole big enough in the side for the horses to enter and fenced around it. Technically it isn't abandoned, but still interesting to document.

Two-story log cabin used for hay barn. It is gone now.

Stone foundation on the two-story log cabin used for hay barn.

Above: Square nails.

Left: This is the two-story log cabin losing the battle before they took it down.

Retired railroad cars must have been easy to get back in the day. I have spotted a few of them that people have parked on blocks and used for storage. They may have been used for grain for a while, but mostly I see lumber, old lawnmowers, and tires.

Few chicken houses are still left out there even though the chicken is growing in popularity in these parts. Farm fresh eggs are so good. But the old round ones of the past are nearly all gone. Some got turned into children's playhouses and others just got to be a garden shed or storage. There is even a house that got turned into a chicken house.

All the farms had to have a place to take the extra goods they produced. The creameries were some of the first structures, as were the elevators in small rural towns. Both were built to be very sturdy. Quite a few of the original creameries are still standing, but many are abandoned, perhaps being used for storage.

This is one big, fancy chicken coop!

Creamery in Alden, MN. Not totally abandoned, as I think it is used for storage, but unless it gets some care it might not last much longer either.

This was in Walters, MN, but I am not sure of its main purpose when built. Possible creamery.

Hayward, MN, elevator. It has been razed.

Others do have someone taking care of them from time to time. Some others are left to crumble. The elevators have sections they use and other parts that sit empty, but many are just torn down. The rust on the old tin makes for some very nice pictures. If it is a rainy day, the rust colors really pop.

All farm children needed schools to go to as well. Small-town schools used to have many children racing up and down the halls. As the farms were abandoned, the kids got to be fewer and fewer until there weren't enough going to the schools to keep them funded. One by one, the schools consolidated to fill up classes and kids had to ride the bus longer to get to school. The school in Emmons was used for a while as a restaurant and even held high school reunions, but now it sits empty like so many others. A couple of old one-room schoolhouses are still around, either converted to a house, used as a studio for artistic endeavors, or yet again

Schoolhouse.

more storage. The windows on these small buildings is usually what give away their identity. They must have needed lots of windows because of the lack of electricity when built, so the light would be plentiful. Most of them added electricity when it became available, but retained all the windows for glorious light to shine in. I feel very lucky when I spot one of these places, but most of them have not survived.

You can tell that people were very imaginative back when it was necessary to use every bit of material available. Nothing got thrown away. Often, I see patches made of tin-can tops and license plates screwed or nailed over a hole in the wall. The lucky children with creative dads were treated to their very own playground equipment made from tractor seats and worn out axles too used up to be on a "working" piece of equipment. Reusing wood and even nails was common practice, so it isn't unusual to see many different types of materials used to build a small shanty or doghouse.

Country schoolhouse turned in to a rental home. It is now vacant and going downhill fast. The tire swing made a great frame!

Built-in cabinets.

Round roof barn. I can see this on my ride to work every day. So many barns between home and work have disappeared. This one will eventually follow.

Another shot of the house near Wells, MN. It was sagging a lot in the middle.

If you look closely, you can see the wall missing toward the middle of the house. The floor has caved in.

Looks like the porch gave way and the house is slowly following.

One of two houses again on the same acreage, except both were old. This one had a date in one of the peaks that said 1910. It and the other house have been taken down and a big new house has been built in their place.

Roofs built to last won't if not kept up!

Left: I just love finding and photographing old doors. It makes one wonder just how many times people came and went through them.

Below: So many textures in so much time.

Love the tin pressed to look like brick.

Tin covered barn.

Partial reflection

Right: One pane at a time disappearing.

Below: Faded paint on an old service garage in Walters, MN.

Roofless house in Walters, MN.

The holes in a straight line on the siding of this house makes me think they used the spray in kind of insulation. Must not have been enough to make the people stay.

Leaning outhouse.

Just a little shed out in the middle of nowhere.

This house was huge! It had so much beautiful trim on all the windows, doors, ceilings, and along the floor.

A child's toy typewriter gathering rust.

This door is almost completely unhinged!

FINAL NOTE

In closing, I want to say I hope you enjoyed this book. My feelings run very deep when it comes to these old abandoned places. They helped us take root in this space, speak to us through time, and show us the power of nature. It is so important to keep these places above ground to remind us of days gone by and help bring back good memories for the generations that once lived in these houses.

I am glad I was able to share my thoughts with you as well as my photos. Please keep your eyes open and listen with your heart as you drive by the weathered farm places of yesterday. If you do decide to stop in to say hello to an old abandoned home, remember, it is very important to be extremely respectful by not taking anything and leaving only footprints behind. "No Trespassing" means just that, and even if a floor looks stable, it could very well be hiding weak spots that are very dangerous. Photos from windows are plenty good. Don't take chances.

ABOUT THE AUTHOR

JULIE BRONSON is a self-taught photographer who loves ambling up and down seldom traveled gravel roads looking for farm places begging to have their photo taken. She can spot an abandoned house from miles away. Her fascination with the architecture of the past never grows old. The beauty of broken down, tired, old, faded wood shows through in the photos she takes. Her photography has been shown in art galleries and other venues in Albert Lea, Owatonna, Austin, and Faribault, Minnesota, and in Clear Lake, Iowa. She can always be found with a camera in hand, recording details of the past to preserve for the future.